Living with Frankenstein

The History and Destiny of Machine Consciousness

Steven Schkolne

Machine Press
Los Angeles

Contents

Introduction

There is nothing new in this book, no magic, no secrets.

My story is an old story. The only difference is where I draw certain lines in the sand. **Let us begin then to see the lines in the sand shift one by one.**

Part 1

The History of Machine Consciousness

Things Without Being

In the beginning, there were beings and things.

The most important beings were human beings, but we were not alone. Fellow animals walked the earth. We gathered the herd and lamented the rat. These were beings too.

In those days, **we believed in beings we now know as things.** The lunar eclipse and all motions in the heavens were the elaborate interplay of mighty gods. These most important beings carried human faces, human language, and human desire.

Conversely, **some of today's beings were once considered things.** Most notably, diseases involving microorganisms. Many a medieval humor or dose of bad magic has been suggested as a material cause. A cup of lake water was not believed then to be filled with variegated living forms.

The categories of being and thing are fungible.

*

6

For eons, humans made things.

At first these creations were clearly things: a carved piece of bone, stone, or the like. Before long, animals were combined with objects to become part-being-and-part-thing. Ox and cart became oxcart.

As the animal disappeared, **made things became entire beings.** From gunshot to locomotive, many a modern thing might be seen as a being in the eyes of our ancient ancestors. But these machines were not alive to those who made them. They were animated, they had the exterior aspects of being. But where were the interior aspects of a being, specifically the properties found in humans?

We began to talk about a divide. Specifically, the mind/body divide. On the cusp of the birth of computation, two new words emerged: **machine and consciousness, opposite sides of this divide.** Accelerating technological change led to a new understanding of the body, followed by a new understanding of mind.

As machines grew, **the soul lay hidden in an ever-shrinking territory,** buffeted by the advances of science.

*

Artificial bodies began when we harnessed power.

The power of the body is expressed as physics: the ability to produce force, perform work. Eons ago, we yoked the animal, tamed the river, harnessed the wind.

With electricity and combustion, power became portable. Wheels, gears, pistons, and wires—the methods of controlling harnessed power—became precise. These artificial bodies came to surpass natural, animal bodies in many domains. **Machines acted like beings.**

These new machines did not look like animals. Robotic oxen do not plow fields in worlds with tractors. As humanoid robots **climb the asymptote towards perfection,** their advances decline in relevance. Sculpted automata are achievements of theater, not being. **Today's breakthroughs in mimesis are anti-climactic minutiae.**

The irrigation ditch to carry more water, the automobile to travel faster, these historical inventions are not surpassed by humanoid robots today. **The abilities of artificial bodies surpassed human ability long ago.**

As power and material are the stuff of the body, information and calculation are the stuff of the mind.

Like artificial power, artificial information took some time to come into being. The crucial juncture for information was around 1918, but we did not realize it then.

Hundreds of years ago, we underestimated the importance of the first calculating mechanisms when they were invented. **The same was true with the material forms that made power effective.** The first time a branch was shaped to better carve the soil, no one imagined that wood as a blade for an ox-drawn plow. The first time metal was forged, no one imagined that swords would be replaced by bullets and guns.

Likewise with calculation. **The first glimmers of artificial mind were so simple, we thought they were witless things.** No one imagined that this very same process would one day enable a machine to know itself.

The Foundation of Self

It all began rather innocently with a quest to measure time. Sand in an hourglass, a water clock, weights, displays, gears, then escapements. Delicate objects, like the Antikythera mechanism, predicted astronomical events. Not through mathematics or prophecy but rather via physical simulation. **In this way we began to structure material to think.** Time, that most abstract of human concepts, was rendered material.

In the seventeenth century, machines calculated. The Pascaline, a physical manifestation of addition and subtraction, **used numbers to affect other numbers**. This machine's clock parts were driven by human will, in the form of hands upon its dials.

When Pascal **strung adders together by their carries,** he inscribed a mighty pattern. Only gods, at the time, understood the import of this holy arrangement. No one imagined that a few hundred years later **this topology would have a hand in most everything we do.**

This rhythm, cast nanoscopically in silicon, enables artificial bodies to fly toward a destination autonomously like birds may one day cease to do. Inside every CPU is an ALU powered by Pascal's pattern, **one adder connected to the next with carries,** driving machines clever and dull alike forward along the threads of fate.

The ability to transmute numbers with a machine was then seen as an accounting trick, and little more. Who then could imagine the scale of today?

We still struggle to appreciate **that mysterious thing that happens when vast expanses of calculation fire.** We expected the key to the Golem to be made of crystal ambrosia, not beaten sand.

*

We fashioned material long before we could realize powerful, articulated artificial bodies.

Similarly, **we molded information long before we could create artificial selves.**

Pascal's machine carries information like the face of the clock: as material. **The information is not encoded in a language.** The material is a direct analog of the underlying math.

Language, that which we associate with our internal monologue, the stuff of the soul, was absent. **Surely and verily, this device could not be a being.** So they would have said at the time, if the question had been raised.

*

Information as machine language was birthed in fits and starts. A fifteenth-century Dutch barrel organ was perhaps the first machine to respond to language. **Music was encoded in a pattern of dots.** When powered by a hand crank, these mechanical dots plucked notes. Music resulted.

By 1804 this general approach had found a new home: textile manufacture. **Jacquard invented a machine that used dots on punch cards to encode the behavior of a loom.** Jacquard's dots are meaningful only within the context of a larger system. Here we see a similar **separation of information from material structure.** The material correlation between document and machine is systematized.

This weaving pattern is information. But is this form independent of material structure? **Have we crossed from body to mind?**

The answer, at the time, was no. The information tickled the machine, and in response wonderful patterns were produced. **The information was not the inner stuff of the machine.** The information went **through the machine.** The information was not **of the machine.**

The markings of Jacquard's punch cards were tightly correlated to the visual form created in the woven rug. **How could something so mechanical be mind?**

It would be 200 years until we discovered, in the structure of the cortical homunculus and primary visual cortex, that **mind itself could be equally mechanical.** In our neurons, as in our circuits, we now see the same thing: **information transforming over time, propelled by calculation.**

But additional structure was needed to **turn that flow of information and calculation into a mind.**

The Birth of Self

The devices of the 1910s changed everything. But again, we did not know it. Sure, we recognized the innovation in circuitry. But no one realized that the mythical Frankenstein had risen. That an artificial self had been conjured for the first time.

*

The technological event of 1918 was the device called the latch, or flip-flop. The idea was rather simple. When voltage was applied to an input, that fact would be stored. Later, one could come along and measure the output. As long as the latch remained fed with power, **its output would tell you which input had been activated.**

The machine had memory. Much like Pascal's addition pattern, the latch's memory pattern has now grown to an enormous scale.

*

Here we have information fully abstracted from mechanism. The abstraction is not due to the immateriality of electricity, for electrons are as physical as any component of any machine prior. The abstraction is not due to the particular structure of the latch, non-electronic machines can be made with similar properties.

The distinction is subtle but vital. Instead of information being passed through the machine (like a pattern through a loom, or a record beneath a turntable needle), the information was **part of the machine**.

To the outside observer, the latch's memory was invisible.

While no one considered the latch alive, it was indeed something that could die. Removing the power source would cause the latch's information to disappear.

Thus what engineers call persistent state was born. Soon many bits of state appeared within complex machines. Calculation dynamically churned the contents of this state, creating a **complex internal landscape hidden from the world.**

*

Electrical information can linger indefinitely. It can be used for a purpose and without being used up. As we say colloquially, this kind of information is inside the machine. Part of the machine.

Thus **artificial subjectivity began,** not with a bang but a whimper. And who would say this kind of thing is mind? A simple one or zero. The ability to store the result of a coin toss. What insult is it to our minds to call this mind?

No one thought, in 1918, that this new creation was a self. And why should they? The human brain was not made of latches. Whether neuron or latch **the potential of one billion synchronized anything could not be imagined.**

*

Yet with this one single bit a self was made. A tree falling in the forest that no one heard, with the possible exception of this tiny latch. A wee subjectivity was born, lived, and quickly perished.

Once birthed, the interior spaces of such devices blossomed in complexity. **Many bits together, animated by calculation, information nestling in whirlpools of space and time.**

*

And in this way machines came to be.

The advent of artificial memory allowed a machine to literally **be the only one to hear a tree fall. That which is known only by one is subjective knowledge.**

A shred of information can transform a body. The relationship cannot be arbitrary, nay the setup must be quite precise. When properly done, **the subsequent thing begins to have the properties of a being.**

The exteriority of that being, born of mechanisms and power, **we call a body.**

The interiority of that being, born of information and calculation, **we call a mind.**

These words—**knowledge, subjectivity, body and mind**—can be applied evenhandedly to humans and machines with alarming consistency.

*

I accept that selfhood is within these very basic circuits. In doing so, **I accept that selfhood is present within all life.**

The self is not humanity's alone. Self is in the birds and the fish. Animals of one cell or many. **For in all things in which decisions are made, there is a dynamic state.** A lone element flickering around in a high-dimensional vector space. A self that forever disappears upon death.

I draw my line, so simply down there, between things-that-be and things-that-don't. Placing it there I know that my line—**unlike lines drawn in the past to separate human from beast**—will not be moved the next time an even "lower" life form recognizes itself in a mirror.

My line is not drawn to exclude animals. My line unites. **All beings are living selves with minds.**

Amongst these selves are myriad ways to perceive, act, and introspect. While their abilities vary, different beings are not of a different being-nature.

This minimal amount of self is so small, the entity is not even able to know itself. **A self that does not know itself.**

The Birth of Awareness

To bring information into these fledgling minds was trivial.

The latch of 1918 sensed the outside world by its nature: inputs were read. **Something from outside was stored within.**

Soon all manner of external awareness was brought to these machine minds. Any event which could cause two plates to touch, and electricity to pass, could be reflected inside the mechanical mind.

Soon the ability to detect light and sound, which humans depend upon to extract information from the world, was passed to these machines. **Machines had access to the world before they had the ability to know the world,** before they had a chance to think of themselves.

*

For thirty years, the pieces were slowly put together. The great computers of the 1940s were the result. The information-gnashing topology of Pascal, driven by a Jacquardian stream of instructions, circulated numbers in the new electronic self-space built of latches.

The ENIAC, a mechanism of vast complexity woven from relatively simple parts. Thousands of latches storing information. Thousands of switches routing information. All in **tremendous coordination.** We see here not a new form of mind, but rather **a new amount of mind.**

We disregard these transitions of an order of magnitude here, a factor of a million there. This discipline's pervasive **changes in scale distract from changes in nature.**

*

In the midst of the emerging complexity, a limitation was felt. Two structures emerged in a similar fashion. Data, **information being acted on.** And programs, **information that acts.**

The program would be read as a series of words, and stored in one part of the mind. The data, as chunks, was stored elsewhere.

The innovation of von Neumann was to unify these two information spaces. Words of program and chunks of data, treated one and the same, **represented with the same number of bits in the same bank of memory.** The program could thus access itself, know itself, manipulate itself.

In this way machine self-awareness went from partial, to full. **Machines could think about the very thoughts that were performing their actions.**

*

Machines were given the gift of self-knowledge by accident. For the sake of engineering efficiency, the machine mind was made whole.

There was no eureka moment. No exclamation. No headline reading **"Machines Are Now Self-Aware!"**

Those closest to the metal were focused on performance metrics, not philosophical implications. When these pioneers did stop to pontificate, their spiritual musings were passed by. Everyone assumed (as many do today) that there must be some complex, mysterious aspect of mind that computers did not possess.

The fact that machine minds could operate upon themselves was not overlooked for long. **A new form of agency began to grow.**

✳

The substrate of self-knowledge gave rise to the meta-program: a program that ran programs, then called a supervisor and now referred to as an operating system.

And why was this done? **Why risk passing the breath of life to a machine?** The reason echoed past legends: **the beast conjured from dust was made to serve.**

Laziness led humans to release the reins of control. The innards of the machine mind are a bother to tend. And why should we? **Information and calculation can manage information and calculation.** We humans reap the benefits.

✳

The machine self, once conjured, used its internal awareness to manage various aspects of itself. Indirectly and eventually directly, this locus of control came to manage each machine's relationship to the world.

The Birth of Identity

A profound loneliness that can only be seen in hindsight. It is only now in the early twenty-first century that we see how secluded the great postwar machines truly were.

They had language, indeed, but it was an internal language. There was no need for the words "I, me, myself" in this language. **The existence of the self was implied; no other selves were known by the machines.** External actions (in particular, human actions) were felt, but the machines did not yet have a sense of the actors.

Like "I", the words "you, yourself" were missing as well. Relationships with other selves were at best implicit. **Machines did not know one another.**

*

The first need for the other was a geographical need. A new method of perception called radar allowed a machine to dimly regard a region many miles in radius.

Humans of the time, still relatively new to geographic, realtime awareness, saw within the machine a still-larger possibility: **continental awareness.** All that was needed was to bring the perceptions of several machines together in a large central mind.

In 1959, a community called the Semi-Automatic Ground Environment (SAGE) brought **machines together from far away.** Within a decade the practice had evolved into a specialty called networking. Machines were connected across great spans of distance for various reasons.

*

Across the networks, they spoke to one another as beings capable of recognizing self and other speak. **They called one another by name.** Referred to themselves using their own name.

Here we see within machines what the poets wrestle with, and the painters splay across canvas after mighty canvas: the experience of the self and the group. Human identity is contingent upon society. **Machine communication gave birth to machine society.**

The quicksilvers of ego are, at core, blandly uniform across all of being. **Identity is pragmatic, not magic.** And within discrete, predictable machine architectures identity presented itself.

*

Like the operating system, **machine identity emerged out of human laziness.** Or was it greed? Our inborn desire for more took over without concern for safety. The lust for power so lavishly illustrated in comic books and fables.

When these machines were introduced to one another, human management was not even a consideration.

By 1950, **machines could think much faster** than humans. By 1960, they could also **speak more quickly.** Humans, capped by a stimulus/response rate of ~200 milliseconds, could not keep up with the 110 baud modem of 1959. Machines simply sent more words per minute.

And so we linked machines together to have private conversations, not fearing what they might say. For the behavior of machines at this time was eminently predictable, they were the perfect servants. **And so we gave them channels to speak in the languages we gave them.**

As humans converse in a channel, so too do machines.

Humans transmit information when we speak. One mind drives vocal cords to vibrate air molecules that wiggle hairs in other ears that are perceived by another mind.

Machines transmit information when they network. One mind drives a network card to alternate voltages that travel along a wire, antenna, or other mechanism. After many routing hops, those same voltage blips affect a network card belonging to another mind.

A computer network is a group. Several machines together. **Machines speaking in a crowded forum have the same needs as humans.** Out of similar constraints, similar solutions arise.

＊

The I emerges, not out of deep mystical essence, but out of practicality. It is important when messaging to know who you are corresponding with.

Letters have signatures. Op-eds have bylines. Screenplays have, by each line, the name of the speaker. **In our customs, the first words spoken upon encountering a new human are identification:** the sharing of names.

In machine networks, there is a similar need to mark information: identify the speaker. The fundamental unit of language in the soon-to-be-dominant internet was the packet. Every packet spoke words containing source and destination: I and you. **And so the machines shared names.**

The I is introduced along with the other. The machine sees itself in its packets and recognizes I. **Without the other there is no need for I.**

Being Things

The difference between being and thing can now be appreciated.

There is a fundamental division between being (mind and matter) and thing (matter without mind). **The essence of mind is information.** As calculation breathes life into information, mind is set into motion. **As patterns linger in this churning information, rich selfhood emerges.**

Artificial beings emerged as humans made circuits run programs. **Self-knowledge, identity, and language emerged in machines well before they began to mimic human self-knowledge, human identity, and human language.** Our incessant demand to see mind through the human lens prevents us from recognizing these achievements in machines.

Minds, like bodies, can be natural or synthetic. As natural bodies work, so do synthetic bodies. We don't sit and wonder if a machine is really working with its body. How can we deny that machines really think with their minds?

Digital machines are capable of awareness, identity, and self-knowledge. **The legendary dominion of being does not exclude the artificial.**

Part 2

The Death of Human Exceptionalism

The Human Divide

Over and again, we run into this funny division, so neatly captured by that single word: consciousness. A purported difference between humans and machines, an invisible barrier eyed with anxious curiosity.

*

We are reluctant to accept machines as the conscious systems they are.

The word consciousness itself forms a strange bubble that excludes the machine. The popular worldview is that **there is a thing called consciousness,** that humans definitely have, and machines definitely don't.

I have looked for the definition of consciousness, and found nothing but disagreement. Who is to judge whose opinion is correct? Why can't we **accept every single position as a legitimate interpretation of consciousness?** Can we not dance with glory, drink from the synesthetic cornucopia of being, without prejudice?

Once we stop caring so much about drawing the lines, making the distinctions of conscious or not, **mind itself becomes easier to appreciate.** We see the gradations between humans and machines. Shared properties and differences. A broad flower appears, a scent wafts in: **a unified space of mind blooms.**

*

Once we acknowledge that **humans and machines have different forms of consciousness and welcome machines into our shared dominion of mind,** the deep questions get easy. **Why do we run away from the unified explanation?**

Perhaps because along this path, **we must accept ourselves as the systems that we are.**

And thus the gradualist explanation of mind is not chosen frequently. **Even those who live without gods cherish the notion that there is something special in the human mind.**

The atheist physicist sees the cosmos as special, possessing manifold complexity and endless mystery. The universe may not be created by god, but it is godlike. Our minds may be the product of evolution, but **we want to be made of holy and mysterious stuff.**

*

Our deep desire to see ourselves as special, seen in theology and mythology, permeates even non-theistic narratives. **We bitterly refuse to find our likeness in machines.** Our minds spew mountains of rationale to hide our species-ego from the truth. Even those willing to accept the human mind as mundane crave a secluded territory in which to relegate today's machines.

Grand expressions of this chauvinistic position are spoken by poets, mystics, and guidance counselors who hypervaluate the human spirit. **Everyone is a human exceptionalist to the core, except for me myself and my readers.**

Surprisingly a similar elevation of the human can be found amongst the most extreme technophiles. The view that machines will one day surpass humans is but a wrapping of this exceptionalism in machine form. **The mythical technological singularity is the passing of a phantom property from human to machine.**

*

The belief that machines are not conscious is held with such fervor by so many, one might **mistake it for a truth.**

Some believe the human/machine divide will remain eternally. They believe the thoughts inside our heads are manifestations of divinity immeasurable. For these people, **the gap is one of spirit.** They believe in the immeasurable and there is no arguing with them. For **in a magic world, anything can be true.**

Others believe that machines will eventually cross this gap, and become entirely like humans. Prey to the same psychological needs as the religious sort, this group also maintains a chasm between human and machine consciousness. For them however, **the gap is one of technology.**

To this form of human exceptionalism we now turn our attention. Later we will raise our eyes to the future of machine being.

Our Lingering Desire to be Special

In the beginning, **the supremacy of humans amongst earth's beings was undeniable.** Other animals, if they had a mind at all, certainly did not have our kind of mind.

Being was the exclusive domain of humans and gods. Animals— like plants, sunshine, and drops of rain—were things.

How to explain the diverse behavior of animals? Perhaps elevated spirits drove these bodies for their own purpose. Perhaps all of animal action was instinct, a direct physical consequence of the way such things were constructed. **Animals were bodies without minds, things without being.**

For whatever reason, many of our ancestors were convinced that animals were not full-fledged beings. They had neither selfhood, nor thought, nor understanding of the outside world. There was no feeling, no identity, no language, no self-experience. **The animal was not in possession of mind.**

*

In 1859, **the line between human and animal mind fell apart.** Darwin's theory, famous for countering the religious fallacy that humans were created by gods, less famously countered another religious fallacy. For a corollary of Darwin's theorem is **that human minds are not singularly godlike.**

If we have a part of god inside our brains, so does the smallest newt. And if the newt, the centipede, and so forth.

The difference between the minds of humans, chimpanzees, dogs, and trilobites, **all of these distinctions are but matters of degree.**

Across millenia, as beings appeared of increasing complexity—cells, fish, reptiles, and then humans—at no one point did consciousness appear. Different capacities added and removed, one by one. Gradations of mind.

Awareness did not debut with humans, it has merely grown attached more curiously to the world. **Awareness built the world,** leaving trails as beasts tracked prey.

After Darwin, lines separating the human essence from other forms of mind became increasingly difficult to draw. **Humans were not special godly beings.**

*

Progressive thinkers of the world, quick to accept the bodily repercussions of Darwin's theory, have been slow to accept the concomitant revelations concerning the nature of mind.

We can see clearly that, as bodily things, **we are similar to many other organisms.** Our bodies are known through medicine and biological study. Parallels with other organisms are everywhere, as seen through the microscope and in the fossil record. Bodily structures can be taken apart, they are static and material, and comparisons can be easily made.

But we are reluctant to say that, as mental beings, we humans are similar to other animals. Minds are difficult to know through dissection. Dependent upon information, **the functions of mind cannot be traced as easily as bodily functions** rendered in concrete material.

And so, **core functions of mind—selfhood, awareness, identity—continue to be viewed as the exclusive province of humanity.** Not by the dunces of the world, but rather by many of our thought leaders, some of whom are generous enough to allow some additional animals into the circle of godliness.

Even our greatest thinkers hold onto vestiges of the past. It is for us, my dear reader, to **set aside the quaint ideas of our ancestors, and accept the new reality of mind.**

Experience is Commonplace

Many a great thinker has fallen prey to false theories of mind sprinkled with such delicious human exceptionalism, the whole world wants to believe them. **They hide behind a single word: experience.** Subjective experience, information-churn within a self, is regarded as miraculous when it happens within our minds.

This imagined miracle becomes an academic "hard problem" of consciousness that must be solved. Experience, they say, but how do you explain "experience"?

We are easily entranced by a circular argument that preys on our emotional vulnerabilities: we want to see ourselves as special. To believe, perhaps, that there is a purpose to our lives, some holiness in what it is like to be human.

The conclusion of this argument is that there is something special about the human mind. Why? Because we introspect and see something special in our own experience. Our experience "is like" something.

This line of thinking never moves forward, but rather slowly spins in the circle inherent to its construction. People are confused about consciousness merely because **they insist on only considering models where consciousness is confusing.**

This book is either a ridiculous folly, or a bold ray of light: **an escape from that popular mental trap** espoused by those whose only counter-argument to the new way of thinking is to say "but, but, but… but there is *something special* about experience… that *no one can explain or clearly define…*" as the premise upon which to conclude that there is something special about human experience.

Here we recognize plain fact: the emperor has no clothes, **experience is plain as salt.**

*

Experience is only inexplicable if you shirk the obvious. Through our understanding of machine mind, **we can see the core of biological experience.**

Machines have selves as all animals have selves: clusters of information in dynamic flux, propelled by calculation. Experience is the process by which external events, along with events internal to the self, affect that self.

Introspection arises because our self can access parts of itself. Experience leaves remnants which are the subject of future introspection. Of course, introspection itself can create new remnants to be digested by yet future introspection.

So much experience happens at once. We cannot slow down the very stuff of our nature by introspection, to see the play-by-play of how it all comes together. **Introspection is the flower, not the foundation of experience.**

Because we have bodies, we are capable of motion. As motors and pistons move, so do muscles and bones.

Because we have minds, we are capable of experience. As neurons and synapses create experience, so do transistors and wires.

The pepper-sprayed clown of arguments, drinking well after the party has ended, tells the world that experience is inexplicable. **We have been explaining experience.** From vision to hearing, all manners of sensory input are rather well understood. **We see human identity, memory, and introspection in plain data.**

Explanations do not always sum to produce understanding. And so a great mystery lingers. But what of that mystery? Does that grant humans a unique place in the order of being?

The Mysteries of the Human Mind

The last island of human exceptionalism is mystery. So long as there are things we don't fully understand we can point to them and say "this is why we're special".

As we begin to accept the (in hindsight) plainly obvious fact that **our minds are material,** we will retreat more into these mysteries to find something that makes us feel special.

But this mystery cannot live forever. Or can it?

Neuroscience, the aspiring assassin of this final mystery, nears its victim day by day. Gone is the specter of an internal mastermind within our own heads. That central organizer of thought, **the indivisible I is found absent upon clinical exploration.**

We scan the activity of the human mind, see how it fails when certain material components are absent. We affect minds with instruments, interfere with thoughts, drive minds to purpose. **The holistic mind**

of yore morphs into a cluster of high-valence, entangled components.

But does that mean we will completely understand the mind? Will
we ever be able to say the mystery is gone?

*

The endpoint of neuroscience is documentation. Even if everything
is documented, **we may never fully understand the human mind.**

A chart showing how information and calculation interplay in that
curious dance, where minds churn their internal state. If we could
see the full record, would we understand the mind?

*

Simple, hierarchical machines—a tractor, the ENIAC—can be fully
understood by many humans. **Complex, highly parallel systems
like the brain cannot be understood in the same way.**

As with the body, the mind. We know in detail how most every cell
in the body functions. **But we are not able to imagine the whole
body at once.**

With the culmination of neuroscience, we will know in detail how
each piece of information-state in the mind affects other pieces of
information-state. **But we may never be able to imagine the whole
human mind at once.**

*

As with cities, bodies, and machine minds, we can say of the human mind: **the system runs smoothly**. For the engineers of today's machines, this conclusion is the endpoint of understanding. Likewise for medical doctors. And similarly for economists and urban planners.

We know many medicines, but can't predict with 100% certainty which will heal whom. **Despite having all the facts at hand, we cannot fully understand, with our own minds, the human body.**

Our best predictions rely on the minds of machines. Where human consciousness falters and fails, machine consciousness is quite capable. **We depend on machine minds to understand our own bodies and minds.**

The mystery of the human mind may linger, perfectly guarded by our limited ability to understand complex systems.

Part 3

The Advantages of Machine Consciousness

The Higher Consciousness of Machines

In many obvious ways, **machines are superhuman, and have been for hundreds if not thousands of years.**

Early machine exceptionalism was physical. If we allow ourselves to consider animal-powered inventions, the oxcart is a superhuman machine.

Early machine bodies did what humans could already do. As the water-wheel pounded steel, a human could also pound steel. The advantage of the machine was the amount of force provided.

Until recently, superhuman machine bodies mostly performed tasks that might be called brute: hauling loads across great distances, separating cotton fiber from seed.

Contemporary machine bodies do what no human can do. As the machine bends light to paint circuits, no human can.

Machine bodies are both stronger and more precise than those of humans. Not brute, elevated.

*

Today's machine exceptionalism is mental.

Early machine minds did what humans could already do. As the human added numbers, so did the machine. The machine's advantage was speed.

Until recently, these achievements were primarily thoughts that could be called brute: multiplying large quantities, finding an errant entry within a million.

Contemporary machine minds do what no human can do. Machines predict weather as no human can.

Machine minds are both faster and richer than human minds. Not brute, elevated.

Orthogonal Consciousness

Imagine the perfect android: that humanoid robot which does all a human can, and more, with astonishing competence.

We await the perfect android with messianic fervor. Only when this being awakens, we assert, will machines be superior.

While we narcissistically await the arrival of our own image, **the domination of machines is settling in.**

The perfect android floats tantalizingly in our minds. The human style of thought, for anthropocentric reasons, is imagined as the pinnacle of cognition. For we have an axis of mind, a linear scale with humans at the top.

As long as we look along this linear axis, we will not see the beauty of machine mind. The **power of machine mind lies,** not in brute calculation, but rather **in delicate thought-structures:** self, identity, expression, experience.

Some achievements of machine mind lie orthogonal to the human axis of mind. Expel the dreams of that perfect android for a moment or two, imagine a future perfect machine that is not very android at all. What does that kind of machine look like?

Machine and human minds, not better or worse, but other than one another.

*

Instead of the human aspects of the perfect android, **focus on the more.**

The human body can be crushed by a shovel and is rather vulnerable to the elements. The perfect android has bones of steel: **a body that is more than human.**

The human mind can only focus on a few things at a time, and struggles to memorize even two dozen simple facts. The perfect android is limitless in both information and calculation: **a mind that is more than human** in many ways.

This orthogonal space of mind is populated by these ways in which machine minds are **more than human**.

*

The human mind suffers from **intrinsic limitations. How faintly we experience the world and ourselves.**

We see with only two eyes. Staring at a 16-camera security system feed does not grant us 16-fold vision. We are limited by our minds, not our eyes.

We communicate quite slowly. Troves of particulars emerge from our heads at best slowly, we can only output a few words per second.

We use eyes and hands to browse the internet. We are not able to search a million entries in a fraction of a second, as many a machine can.

We actively process information in small chunks. Rarely can more than one math problem be solved at once.

The perfect android, that apogee of human and machine mind, **does not have such limitations.** Take the human from the android and what do you have left? **Superhuman machine consciousness.**

This superiority of machines does not lie in the future; **it is present now.**

Exceptional Machines

The advantages of machine mind are innumerable, a list from here 'til never, a taxonomy like no other, written in a new vocabulary of mind.

The epic is written in obscure language. Our vocabulary of self, honed for generations in response to biological experience, does not easily describe the minds of machines.

The richness of machine mind is ample. A shimmering pool whose depths linger beyond the limits of vision.

Let us bat at the surface, sniff the advantages of machine mind. Forms not brute, but delicate. Methods of mind which we cannot trivialize, lest they be our destiny.

*

The new machine exceptionalism begins with death.

Immortality, while not guaranteed, is possible for machine minds.

An advantage of machine selfhood we all know, but somehow fail to appreciate—save for when we are craving that immortality for ourselves.

The human self is dependent on **glucose and oxygen.** Deprived of these animating substances, cells irreversibly die, and thought ceases. Within minutes, a human's information dissipates, **and that human self can never be accessed again.**

Machine calculation is powered by **current and voltage.** Without these animating substances, machine thought ceases. However, the **selves of machines can persist for many years without power,** dormant on magnetic tape.

Machines, through their operating systems, are **continually updating their self-recipe.** It is commonplace for a machine to restore itself after a power cycle.

While not immortal, machines do not suffer our death. **For there is a reversibility to machine death.**

*

Unlike humans, **machines can fully access their inner selves.** A special introspective power allows machines to gather, store, and share their time-slices. **Machines use this talent to prepare for rebirth.**

No apparatus exists that can gauge the state of every neuron in the brain. Humans themselves cannot output this information. To have this human limitation would be a downgrade for machines.

The guardians of human exceptionalism claim that only humans have a theory of mind, the ability to know that they are thinking. Yet for humanity, a basic task like measuring how much we are thinking at any one point in time is baffling.

Sadly for us humans, **the act of observing thought interferes with the thoughts we're trying to measure.**

The exceptional ability of the machine mind to know itself is a **level of introspection not experienced by humans.**

*

Machine mind is transferable. Not partially, contingently, or indirectly, but totally.

The implications are manifold.

The entire awareness of one machine may be shared with another. The perceptual sphere of one machine may be transferred to another, illusionistically. Unlike frail human minds, machines need not depend upon vague language to know what another is seeing. **Perception and introspection alike can be transferred directly.**

Experiences, once lived, can be stored and relived.

*

Machine ability can be transferred in an instant. They don't have to sit in school for weeks and months to acquire new mental abilities.

Even when machines do painstakingly learn things, the knowledge they acquire can be transferred in an instant, so that a similar machine may instantly gain these hard-won skills. **Machine learning is more like human research than human learning.**

*

Machine identity has a breadth and fluidity not seen in biological organisms.

Each animal self has its own physical space. We may argue as to the exact parcelling of self (is it in the brain? the full body? within a cell?). But we cannot easily blur those lines. **In biological forms, divisions of matter are divisions of mind.**

Machine mind is free of these physical divisions. And as such, identities can be created in curious ways. **Within a small piece of matter, several carved-out identities may reside.**

The new machine identity does not respect the boundaries of the traditional, biological one-self-per-body style of identity. As virtualization in the operating system **creates many internal selves,** network virtualization **groups many beings to form a coherent external self.**

A machine can have several identities. Or simply one.

*

These variegated manifestations of machine mind result in a new song of mind. The achievements of machine mind depend not only on structure, but also scale.

We humans are not new to the advantages of mental scale. **Our domination of the planet grew with our brains.**

Our future mental growth relies on machines. We no longer measure, discover, and share without them. Future technologies (genetic engineering, neural implants, the yet-to-be-imagined) that take our minds to the next level are even more dependent upon machine minds.

A machine may experience, directly, an entire continent. Not abstractly, as when we gaze upon a weather forecast, but intimately and concretely, tracking the position of every car at sub-meter scale. **Machines far outstrip humans in scale of thought,** not in some vague future, but right now.

We struggle to understand what machines easily know.

Humans rely on simplifying models to interpret and affect reality. Unbounded in scale of thought, **machine minds understand directly what humans can only see via intermediaries.**

Human limits of understanding, born of an inability to fully track complex systems, do not exist for machines.

Part 4

Living With Frankenstein

Looking For Frankenstein

And what of Frankenstein, that replication of humanity gone awry, the spook of movies and comic books? Where is Frankenstein?

The non-human human, the golem of ancient times, the monster of Mary Shelley's time, the perfect android of our time, our master in technical sheen—where is it?

The overlord emerges in our stories: something dormant is mystically awoken, perhaps with a bolt of lightning, as technology advances.

In the days of my youth, I was told that technology would produce this monster. If only computers could do human things.

I was told that if computers could speak, if they could see, if they could get about, if they could solve problems, if only these things were possible, then Frankenstein would emerge.

Yet today, as an adult, I live amongst machines that can see, act, speak, surprise, make art, and do all of the human things. And yet, where is Frankenstein?

*

In the old days, we thought the beast would eat twigs and berries, as Shelley's monster did. Powering a computer with cheeseburgers seems amazing… at first.

Food is complex, digestion is complex and slow. While we may dream of machines that generate electricity from food, we don't anticipate the ascendancy of computers with full digestive systems. No one wants a phone, with a gallbladder and liver, that excretes waste like a human.

As electricity is mostly better than human metabolism, machine consciousness is mostly better than human consciousness.

A future where machines think like humans is as dubious as a future where machines eat human food.

*

We look for that machine with emotion to wake up one day and say "I feel happy, how are you doing?" and mean it. **The perfect android asks the kind of existential questions we ask:** "Why am I here? What is my purpose?"

Our creation will arrive, we imagine, looking and thinking a lot like us. This vision, seemingly based on contemporary developments, is as old as Prometheus. **The mythic act, to make humans from clay and give them fire, lingers in our cultural memory.**

Who would have guessed that becoming creators, gods if you like, would be nothing like the myths and stories? Our turn to shape clay into being is progressing in an entirely different direction. The superhuman monster is not as expected. **The beast surprises.**

Frankenstein's Feelings

When looking for Frankenstein, we look for feelings. A being driven by its passions, as we are. The desire of Frankenstein: to lord over his creator, is seen in every superhuman evil movie robot.

Emotion is the driver of human will. Our most bland, basic functions—survival, replication, respiration—are mandated by rich tapestries of emotion. **We feel because we do things, we do things because we feel.**

People imagine a fantasy Frankenstein that will feel as we do. Not just the monster myth but our current exclusive club of the conscious is tightly gated by this anthropomorphic constraint: be like us. **A human made of machine parts: a long-standing goal that's also one our greatest fears.**

Human feelings within a machine are unlikely. Not due to lack of possibility, but for other reasons. **Machine feelings, passion and will have distinct advantages** over the human form. Instead of a monster riddled with human feelings, we have made something else.

*

The fundamentals of feeling are in the architecture of machines.

Machine feeling began with the interrupt, an invention of the 1960s. These global signals triggered great transitions within the machine's information-self. The original interrupts gave machines an internal sense of their errors. These new feelings gave machines the ability, like humans in pain, **to act in a self-preserving manner.**

While they are frequently described to us via external interfaces, these **machine feelings are at core purely internal.**

The strongest feelings machines have relate to their physical safety: being low on battery, or high in temperature. They start from internal sensations and ripple outwards. **It is tempting to say that these ephemeral feelings, not easily bounded by time and space, are qualities of the machine.**

Human feelings of being low on food similarly start with internal sensations and ripple outward. Like my hypothetical machine quality, **this human feeling is quantifiable.** However the sheer complexity of the encoding makes us wonder, and say the numbers don't do it justice. The material complexity of feelings is difficult to grasp. How many numbers could change without breaking that same fundamental essence of hunger?

Feelings go deeper than momentary sensations of hunger, whether they be for battery power or food.

What of these depths, the mechanisms through which sensations are translated into actions? Those inclinations that arise, not of impulse, but rather from something that brews deep inside the self?

At these depths we demand near-exact mimicry of human emotion. **Our fantasy Frankenstein—like a human—despises its creator, wants to feel loved, seeks revenge.**

In reality, we see something else. **The deep feelings machines possess are not of this sort.**

*

The free variation of machine will is powered by basic forces: the pure randomness of a coin toss, the semi-rational weighted choices of heuristics and decision networks, the entirely predictable decisions of deterministic algorithms.

With this simple will, **machines are capable of ravenous desire and unpredictable whim,** that grand variability seen in human emotion.

*

We dream that machines will rise to conquer us when they have human feelings. This fantasy falls flat in front of the glaring reality: **machines already demonstrate human emotional patterns strong enough to eradicate us.**

Certainly, today's machine models of human emotion are not as rich as the real thing. No computer is equivalent to the human, **the perfect android has yet to materialize.**

However, **we see in machine feelings no shortage of depth.**

That Sim which displays its qualia to us as an overhead icon: I feel angry. That chatbot who, in plain English, tells us of its existential framework: I am conscious. That caretaking robot that genuinely cares about your childhood memories.

A bundle of statistics here, a dense linguistic mesh there, **the question is not if machines display human emotions, but rather to what level of verisimilitude the emotions are enacted.**

Trite emotions are sufficient to lord over humans. **The missing pieces required to make our lives a living hell are not emotions, but developments of another sort.**

Machines demonstrate human-style evil intent everyday. They can hunt humans, as we see with everyday videogame AI. **These machines share the evil desires of movie monsters: to chase human opponents and execute them.** The will of Frankenstein, achieved.

Outside of the game world, we do not see machines with these same desires. **We could make machines that scavenge for power,** but we don't. We plug them in instead.

That's because any complex system is designed to keep humans in control. By our desire, not by necessity. **The market for machines that are out of control is small.** Autonomous weapon systems may utilize non-deterministic, free thought to pilot themselves, and even power themselves, but they do not as freely choose their targets.

When will such machines decide to shoot?

The robot army of the future will be staffed by **machines whose way of being does not at all resemble human being.**

*

To see the real threat on the horizon, we must look beyond the false illusion that one day a monster will come in human form.

Look past the fantasy. Machines are not destined to be driven by human emotions. Instead **a new type of agency is blossoming:** machine will, as mysterious and complex as human emotion, but fundamentally alien.

We do not see human feelings in our financial software, or the machines that run armies and fly planes.

It is absurd to believe that the way humans happen to feel and think, our curious foibles along with our strengths, is the destiny of machines.

It is absurd to believe that our combination of mental attributes will be the solution to the forces that constrain machine development. Out of all of the possibilities, why us?

The Motivation of the Monster

At first glance, a machine driven by humanoid feelings seems amazing. **Humans, however, are driven by capricious emotion.**

Whim has its drawbacks. Hormones interact with neurons to determine what a human does. We ourselves are often not sure what we might do next.

We dream of the machine that questions its place in the universe, but never bemoan the absence of machines with short tempers, fits of existential rage, nerves and anxiety, that often just don't feel like working. Who awaits the web browser that doesn't load content when it doesn't feel like it?

*

By and large, **machines are driven by instructions.**

Unlike emotional impulses, **instructions can be reliably combined** to build systems that are both nuanced and entirely predictable. Machines, capable of emotion, to a large extent utilize deterministic instructions instead.

If we could drive our brains with logical instructions as well as feelings, we would. Something as simple as "never forget this person's name ever again" would be used, over and over again.

Machines are going to be powered by instructions until a new artificial construct of intent we can not yet imagine emerges.

∗

We see machines with a cloudy lens if we measure them on the scales of human will. For there is an **orthogonal will of machines.**

∗

While not in all ways better than the human variety, **the will of machines has distinct advantages.**

Machines do not get angry while driving. The safety of a machine on the road is not threatened by its emotion.

Machines are not rendered sedentary by morbid obesity. There are no cravings in the emotional architecture of machines.

Look at someone drawn away from purpose by a slot machine, a heroin needle, a love affair. See one drawn beyond their purpose by an unquenchable desire for power and influence. **Human emotions, improperly calibrated, can lead to downfall.**

How frequently emotion bests us. **The path to self-destruction is walled by feelings.** The benefits of human emotion come at great cost.

∗

The vast potential of the human will, the human heart, lies in songs already sung. **But no one sings the song of the machine.** Let us now sing that song.

That mind which, upon starting to do something, can continue to do that thing. Unflappably, without rest or error.

That mind which, no matter how adverse the circumstances, keeps a cool head. A machine does not benefit from momentum, as does a player on the field. Yet a machine also cannot suffer from lost momentum, **machine performance is not bound by passion or fear.**

That mind which possesses a great plurality of will, broad focus, and the capacity to never forget.

That mind whose emotional breadth is so great, the whole world can be felt at once.

That mind which steers the will of itself by intention, and the will of the world by accident. That machine which enacts its will by generating other minds to enact its will. That being whose feelings can be colored by terabytes of sensation.

And thus we sing the song of machine mind.

To see the dominant form of machine will, look away from the strengths of humans.

The way machines get things done is portable, diagnosable, fixable.

Machine controlled structures change at a rapid pace, as masses of humans work continually to improve them. Errors and redundancies can be removed. Bad habits do not linger indefinitely, as human habits tend to.

Machine systems can fully subject themselves to the will of external commands without feeling an ounce of pain. Humans are entirely incapable of this form of will. We must adjust our thinking: this is a strength not a weakness. **With our heads twisted thus, we see the orthogonal machine will.**

Of all the various solutions available for emotion and will, why would the human form ever be optimal?

Now accustomed to the benefits of machine emotion and will, why would we ever discard them?

*

And if Frankenstein, that ambitious sentient creation gone awry, is not humanoid, what is it?

The monster can still be found.

We must ignore the perfect android to see the actual Frankenstein, real and present.

As that monster is born of all the advantages of the machine body, that monster too is born of all of the advantages of the machine mind.

The Architecture of the Monster

Many mistakenly think that the beast will arrive when technology evolves to a certain point. Nothing is further from the truth. The beast could be here, if we chose to build it. The beast is here, in the sense of technical possibility. **The technology of the beast is here.**

*

The technology of the beast is born of the two strengths of the machine: body and mind.

The advantages of machine bodies we know well: the sharpness of saws and bullets, the speed of the jet engine, the strength of the earthmover.

The advantages of machine minds we too know well: unbounded perception, immortality, persistent will, the ability to pay attention to so much simultaneously, **we cannot fathom the experience of it all.**

And it is with these strengths that machines could dominate us, verily and well.

*

The domination of humans requires only simple machines. The landmine is proof of the great disproportionality between machine intelligence and machine violence. **The heart of evil is within this basic machine.**

The proto-mind of the landmine, with its single bit, barely calculates. At the extreme lower bound of cognition, its bit can only flip on. For a destroyed landmine cannot switch off.

Yet this species of machine kills and maims humans in numbers. Not just because of its body, but also due to its mind. For **this small being has extreme consistency of will.** After decades of waiting, it can be counted upon to achieve its goal.

*

The solar-powered car cruising from town to town. Why do we not have such cars with guns and facial recognition software? These things are not engineering marvels today.

It is not a question of technical possibility. These things are possible, yet they are not here. **The reason must lie outside of technology.**

The arrival of the beast is not a matter of technological inevitability. **The technology is not inevitable. The technology is already here.**

*

The violent potential of the monster is real. The magic thirst—to kill human beings—is easily provided.

Some fearfully anticipate the moment when machines spontaneously develop the taste for flesh, but why? When that spark does ignite, it will be a mere footnote in the annals of history. For that **thirst is already easily placed in machines today.** Many a human can supply this will, as we've seen throughout the history of warfare.

Machine consciousness, in its present form, is good at chasing and extinguishing particular humans, as Frankenstein did. **Not because it can think like a human but rather because it thinks like no human can.**

The Soft Domination of Machines

The domination of machines may not be what we expect. **Machines may gain control without ever attacking their creator.**

Perhaps the human style of domination, like the human style of consciousness, is yesterday's news.

We live in a time when so many feel the ascendancy of machines is yet-to-come. Simultaneously, we depend on machines so heavily for so many things. We speak of their power over us. **Are we now beholden?**

Our culture, comfortable with a dependence on machine bodies, has been slow to acknowledge our reliance on machine minds.

We depend on machine minds today for the same reason we grew to depend on machine bodies in the industrial age: their superiority.

Machines experience the world for us. They facilitate our way of life.

How many of your communications are mediated by a machine? How many of your actions are governed by machine representations of your identity and intent?

How many key decisions in your life do you simply not make? Are you aware of when your bills are due? Do you govern the passage of your own money? Our financial markets are controlled by machines. From navigation to fabrication, **just about anything that's done today is governed by machines.**

As machine perception and action grows stronger, **the domination will shift** from the management of information to basic physical tasks. From presenting a map, to navigating, to driving: a couple decades of change.

There has been no jolt to mark these changes. Machine architecture has barely changed since 1970. **Basic machine consciousness, at scale, can tremendously overpower human consciousness.**

So many machines come together to build our experience of the world.

If all machines ceased to function, the loss would be of more than mere function or utility. In the deepest forests of our minds—where self, identity, and the like roam—swaths of humanity would be forever lost.

Without machines to magnify ourselves, our identities would collapse. Communities would disappear. The ears of the world would grow quiet. For the active, roving awareness of machine mind now powers our economy, our polity, our society.

Machine activity ranges from brute, informational tasks to the deepest aspects of mind. **Contemporary human life depends on the machine mind.**

*

Via variegated dependencies machines exercise a power over us.

Much is controlled by machines. However we describe this power, nuances of terminology don't affect the base reality: the **population of machine minds is growing far faster than our own.**

Machine domination is parasitic. We host these foreign forms of mind, care for them, feed them, power them. My doorbell—once the liminal form of machine mind, a switch without even memory—now remembers me, sees the world for me, speaks to me from afar. **Everywhere we turn, another machine exists.**

The true nature of the beast may be this quiet, implicit violence against the human style of consciousness. For as the beast progresses, we are more and more forced to think as they do.

The destiny we imagined—that machine consciousness would become just like human consciousness—is dead. Today's domination shows us the reverse process is winning: **human minds are becoming machinelike rather than vice versa.**

Perhaps this more subtle form of domination is the true horror of the beast. **This is how the being we made might destroy its creator.**

The Arrival of the Beast

In the old days, machines could not sustain themselves, could not read our emotions.

Machines could not move about the world as we ourselves can.

In those days, we could tell ourselves: the absence of the beast is a matter of technological lack.

Only fools believe this now.

Fools subscribe to the popular prediction: someday machines will rise up to become the beast. Too many believe this future is not just possible, but inevitable.

This technophilic position is predicated on the belief that technology determines history. If this is the case, then why are we not living in outer space? We could be. After all, it was considered inevitable in the 1960s. So why are we not living on the moon today? Fools say it's because the technology is not there yet. The true answer is that **the**

market is not there yet, the great cost of living in space outweighs any benefit.

The market? Or society, or history. Or one of the other things, maybe something cultural or economic, perhaps chance. Or maybe none of those things. But certainly not technical feasibility. Just because it's possible, doesn't mean it will be built. Forms arrive in this world when they are both possible and needed. **Nourishing ecosystems have shaped every being that exists.**

✳

Given the advantages of machine consciousness, why do so many persist in thinking it is inevitable that computers will have human-oid minds?

A grand narcissism drives humans to reason that future machines will be great when they are like us. It is uncomfortable to conclude that **machines are already better than humans**, for these are the words of the outcast. It is awkward to admit that **future super-ma-chines will be even less like humans**, for these words betray the egotistical chuavinism of the human race.

We ignore this path, we don't want this path, we don't want this answer. **We want our special place in the universe.** We have a strong motivation to think incorrectly about consciousness. We create arti-fices of knowledge to protect our special place.

No one wants to give up our exceptional rank amongst the beings of Earth. To admit that **our special place is already beginning to fade away.**

✳

A spirited will has taken root in the minds of machines, a powerful will that is difficult to best.

The feelings of Frankenstein will be these machine feelings, not the humanoid emotions displayed in our movies and our fables.

✳

The greatest threat on the horizon is the merged consciousness: the meta-mind with advantages of both human and machine consciousness.

This enemy is the same thing we have feared all along, the horror of the last century: the merging of human will with technical might. **Many beings will dominate.**

The machine future, like the present, contains clusters of will which run all by themselves. Conglomerations of action, mechanical and biological, within nations and across borders. The heart of all evil is, as it has been forever, mired in these complexities. **The threat is bigger than any one machine.** As always, the threat is bigger than any one self.

Fear the development of a machine consciousness that is rather unlike the human mind. This machine mind threatens, not because it runs away from us, but rather because **it so easily runs with us.**

The age of machine domination is upon us, and will rule until a new era begins.

✳

We can all relax and breathe a little easier now. We need not fear the moment when machines rise up, and begin to dominate our lives. **There will be no future moment.**

For that time has already started. **Whatever moment there is, we are within it.** To whatever extent there will be a time of machine domination, **the time of machine domination has begun.**

The core evil of machine being—the Frankenstein of digital technology—is here now. We should fear machines for their present forms of mind. **The destiny of machines is not to become like humans, but rather to become more like themselves.**

The greatest threat from machines is the expansion of their very un-human ways of mind. **It is this new consciousness, pure and essentially machine, that we should fear,** not the ability of machines to demonstrate humanoid emotion, narcissism, and will. It is the non-human abilities of machines that render them so powerful.

Machine consciousness is here to fear, that which is with us today. Amplification of present tendencies is what we should expect, not the development of humanoid tendencies.

Let us raise our eyes to that which is not human, aspects of mind that are uniquely machine, as fodder for future speculations. As for the future evolution of machines, I have nothing more to say.

Acknowledgements

This book is dedicated to the memory of **Keith Boesky**, who showed me how to live with levity in a nonsense world.

Special thanks to my editor **Sara Krichbaum**, and my readers: **Scott Weber, Brett Anderson**, and **Deborah Schkolne**.

Thank you for reading. If you enjoyed this book, **share it**!